e.male
prayers for the lads

Kevin Mayhew

dave gatward

First published in 1998 by
KEVIN MAYHEW LTD
Rattlesden
Bury St Edmunds
Suffolk IP30 0SZ

0 1 2 3 4 5 6 7 8 9

ISBN 1 84003 262 6
Catalogue No 1500225

Cover design by Tim Mountford
Edited by David Gatward
Typesetting by Louise Selfe
Printed and bound in Great Britain

—— Contents ——

For Marti and Trev – The Brow Boys

—— Introduction ——

Right, here it is; a bunch of prayers about being a lad and being a teenager and being confused. It's not an 'I've been there so listen to me!' book, just a collection of thoughts on stuff you're probably going through. There aren't necessarily any answers, but I hope that as you read them you'll realise that God isn't a god who keeps his hands clean. He's a God who gets stuck in with you and where you're at; all you've got to do is get to know him, and that's called 'prayer'.

Cheers,

DAVE

—— Nice pecs! ——

Lord,
    why do people think
    that's it's only girls
    who worry about their figure?
Lads can get bothered about it too, you know.
Whether we're too fat,
    too skinny,
    not muscly enough,
    too small,
    too tall.

So, let's get it right;
    it's not just the girls.

You see, Lord,
    I'm not happy with my body.
Yes, I'm healthy,
    and at least I'm not grossly over weight,
    but I feel . . .
    . . . puny.

I want to be fit, Lord,
    muscular.
Proud to take my T-shirt off.

Attractive to girls.

I mean, just look at me!
Call that a bicep?
And my legs!
Like two sticks of celery.

People tell me not to worry,
    that I look fine, healthy.
But I don't feel it.
I just feel inadequate.

I don't think I'm making a fuss.
My body is something
    I want to keep in good shape.
Having a bit of muscle would help that . . .
. . . and me.

Do you understand, Lord?
I'm not really a sporty person, you see.
Always last to be picked for footy
    or anything else for that matter.
So to have *something* that I was good at,
    something physical I could do
    would make all the difference.
To put some meat on the bones.

I know some say it's vanity,
    but it's not that I'm vain.
I guess I'm the exact opposite.
But if I did get a bit of muscle,
    it wouldn't make me big-headed.
Just a bit happier.

I hate feeling this way, Lord.
I don't want it to become an obsession.
I don't want it to take over my life.
I just want to be healthy,
    and feel a little happier with who I am
    and what I look like.
That's OK, isn't it?

Amen.

—— Boomty boom! ——

Lord,
   she's gorgeous!
She is amazing!

I'm in love!
(I think).

Well,
   I probably wouldn't admit that
   to any of my mates.
After all,
   being 'in love'
   is wussy
   and wet,
   where as we're far too 'cool'
   to be like that.

But she is rather nice, Lord.

Does she like me?
You see,
   I'm not sure,
   and I wondered if
   (as you have
   a rather unique perspective on things)
   you knew.

Well, does she?
You see,
   I've only spoken to her a couple of times
   and any opportunity I do get
   I mess up,

try not to blush
and run away slowly,
all calm and casual,
trying to say, 'Hey, I'm too cool to care!'

Stupid, isn't it?

Fun though.
It is fun this, Lord.
She's lovely,
   I like her quite a lot.
   There's a bit of a chase on,
   rumours,
   all that kind of stuff.
It's great!

So,
   as I sit here,
   at the back of the classroom,
   straining for just a glimpse
   of that straight, jet black hair,
   I just wanted you to know, Lord,
   that I'm happy.

Cheers!

Amen.

—— And the lights are low ——

Relationships are supposed to be good, Lord.
You know,
    fun and stuff,
    something we all should like.

I'm not sure about that anymore.

I've been 'going out' with you-know-who
    for four months now.
(Longest lasting relationship in our year!
Cool, eh?)
It was all going well for a while.
Lots of fun and things.

But then something happened.

I feel so guilty, Lord,
    and confused.
Being a teenager isn't easy,
    especially when you're on your own
    and the lights are low.

We were kissing and stuff, Lord,
    which was nice,
    but we were alone
    and we just kept on kissing.
I felt myself go all hot
    and it started to get more passionate
    I suppose.
We started to touch each other
    and unbutton stuff.
We couldn't help it.
She told me she wanted to go further,

go as far as I wanted,
even all the way.
I said no,
but we didn't exactly just kiss, Lord.

I feel so guilty, and now she wants to do it again.
I'm so confused inside.
I know I shouldn't
but at the same time
I want to.
I want that experience again,
I want to feel that touch.

Lord,
this is so difficult.
I don't know what to do,
or how far to (or not to) go.
I could sit here and talk to you all day about it,
but I've got to confront the situation
and do what I think is right.

This is so hard, Lord.
I don't want her to think I'm rejecting her,
especially as I so want to do it again.
But it could go even further
and that scares me so much, Lord.
That's so much more,
so much deeper,
so much . . .

It's just so difficult!
Why did you give us these feelings?
Why did you give us these drives?
What am I supposed to do with them now?
Like I can control them!
And why should I?

No one else does!
(Well, that's what they say).
So why should I?
What's the point?
It's only natural after all!

It's not that simple though, is it?
No, it's not that simple at all.
It goes much further,
   and I can't help but think that going that far
   is wrong
   and dangerous.
Very dangerous,
   when you think of what could happen,
   or what it could all mean.
I'm only young after all,
   and I can't deal with that!
Not that kind of commitment!

Oh, God!
I hate this!
My mind is so full up
   I wish I had a tap attached
   so that I could at least turn it on
   and let some of this confusion out!

Do you understand, Lord,
   because at times like these
   I need to know that you do,
   even if I don't.

Amen.

—— Breaking up ——

Lord,
    this isn't easy.
No surprise I guess,
    but I still have to say it.

I'm breaking up with her.
Why?
Oh, I don't know.
I'm not ready for anything serious?
I'm not 'in love' with her?
It's just not working out?

All sounds a bit empty, doesn't it?
I mean, Lord,
    how on earth
    am I supposed to say to her
    that it's 'over'?
How do I say it?
What do I say?

I want to run away.
Maybe, if I'm gone long enough
    she'll just forget me
    and get on with her life.
Can't do that though.
Not very fair, really.

This is awful, Lord.
I feel awful because I'm with her
    and it doesn't feel right,
    and I feel awful
    that I have to tell her.
It'd be easier to just keep it going.

You know, don't tell her.
But that's not right.

Thanks, Lord,
   for making this all so easy!
(Not.)

So, this is the process we go through
   until we find the 'one for us'?
Hmmmmm,
I'm not impressed.
Not one bit.
It's hell!
Couldn't you have made it
   a little bit simpler?

No, I guess not.

We did have some fun though.
The disco,
   the picnic,
   the day she pushed me in the pond!

But now it's different,
   and I have to be honest with her.

Help me Lord,
   and her,
   as we go through this . . .

. . . our first 'breaking up'.

Amen.

—— But it tastes of sick! ——

That was revolting!
Sorry, Lord, but it's the truth.
I know I'm supposed to be grown up about this
    but I'm lost for words!
And people drink this stuff for fun?
For recreation, a laugh?
For image?
Not worth it, Lord, well, not this stuff anyway.
I'm sure the only people who drink whisky
    are those so old that all their taste buds
    are dead.

Beer . . . Now, that's a bit different!
Tastes OK to me, and to my mates.
We had a few at the weekend
    out in the garden (not mine, by the way).
It was great, but I must admit
    my head was banging a bit in the morning.
This is only a short prayer, Lord,
    but I just wanted to let you know
    that I don't want to get daft
    when it comes to drink.
Unfortunately, I know I probably will,
    because even though I know that headaches,
    dizziness,
    throwing up and being ill isn't fun,
    the drinking can be.

Help me, Lord,
    so that I don't make a complete idiot
    of myself.

Amen.

—— Prove your age! ——

Lord,
   last night
   a few of us got together.
It was supposed to be just a small party
   but by the end of the night
   it was anything but.
The house was packed,
   most of the people I'd never seen before
   and it didn't finish until about four.

Most of the time it was fun.
Sort of a 'grown-up' feeling
   mixed with a sense of rebellion.
No parents,
   just us,
   having a party.

But a couple of hours later,
   and a few drinks later,
   I felt a little different.

I woke up at two in the toilet.
Apparently I'd disappeared about twelve.
(Nice of everyone to come looking.)
I didn't know anything about it.
To be honest I thought I'd been there
   for about five minutes.

I must have passed out.
But the punch was so nice!
Really fruity and sweet . . .
   . . . I didn't know it had been spiked

and I thought everyone was laughing
because they were having a good time.

Well they were,
    at my expense.
They all knew
    that I didn't know.

I can't remember how much I drank, Lord,
    but this headache
    and sick feeling
    keep reminding me
    that it must have been far too much.

I'm not used to it, am I, Lord?
Well, for a start,
    I'm not old enough either.
I'm just one
    of thousands of teenagers
    excited by the dangerous
    and unknown
    and desperate for a taste.

Was I wrong, Lord?
I guess I was,
    but so many of my friends drink.
Well, they say they do, anyway.
I find myself lying sometimes,
    saying that I had a few drinks here and there
    or whatever.
Stupid, eh?

I'm sorry, Lord.
I don't mean to be so easily led,
    but sometimes

going against the crowd
is so difficult.

I feel sick,
　　hungover,
　　stupid,
　　yet worried I'll do the same again
　　even though I know already
　　what could happen.

I want to enjoy myself, Lord,
　　be happy,
　　have a good time,
　　enjoy being a teenager,
　　but at the same time
　　I'm not too happy about being led so easily
　　and just joining in.

Do you understand, Lord?
You will help me, won't you?
Even if I make the same mistake again?
Thanks.

Amen.

—— Picked last ——

Lord,
    it's freezing.
I'm stood here on icy ground
    a mile away from all the action.
Why do I always get put in defence,
    or goal?
Being picked last
    really hurts at times.
I can't help it – that I'm not that good
    at football.
It's just one of those things.
But every time we play,
    the PE teacher
    allows the 'best players'
    to pick the teams.

I wish they'd just do it randomly.
That way
    even though I'd still end up
    in defence again,
    at least I wouldn't have been humiliated
    and picked last.

Stupid game.
Stupid PE teacher.
Stupid me.

Well, I'm not stupid,
    I just can't play football.
I've never been able to, Lord!
It's a family trait.
Most dads and sons probably kick a ball
around.

Us?
Nah, we never did.
Dad couldn't play
    and neither could we
    so we'd make catapults
    and bows and arrows instead.

Now, Lord,
    were there to be a part of the curriculum
    that included archery or catapult use,
    then perhaps I'd stand a chance.
I could hit a drinks can
    at 50 paces with a single stone
    from my special, handmade,
    'Dad-endorsed' (so it *had* to be good!)
    catapult.

But no.
Those of us who don't enjoy the usual,
    who find football about as interesting
    as watching an egg boil
    are left out.
Time and again it's football,
    then athletics, then more football.

So, here I am,
    standing on a piece of wet grass,
    freezing and bored
    with just one little prayer . . .
. . . could I, just once,
    experience the classroom-gossip joy
    of being a goal scorer?

Cheers.

Amen.

—— Bullied ——

I'm not going to school today, Lord,
   and only you know why.
Only you know the real reason.

I'm not ill,
   though after the phone call
   my teacher thinks I am.
My symptoms are the usual:
   I was really sick in the night,
   I felt really weak,
   and now need today to get over it.
Convincing, eh?

No, not ill;
   just scared.

I'm scared, Lord.
So much so
   that when I think of it
   I really do feel sick.
My stomach tightens and churns,
   I feel shaky
   and then start to panic.

But what can I do?
I'm petrified.
They threatened me and said
   that if I told anyone
   they'd get me.
Beat me up.
Duff me in.
Smash my teeth in.
Kill me.

Do me over.
Break my legs.
Kick my head in.

And some other things.

What am I supposed to do?
I'm so scared.
The school's so big,
   they could get me anywhere,
   and then if I grassed,
   they'd do it again.

What is it with me?
Why are they doing this?
Is it that I'm not a nice person?
It must be
   otherwise they wouldn't do it.
But that's not true, is it?
Other people like me.
So why me, Lord?
Why me?

I want to run away.
Either that
   or retaliate.

Sometimes I dream
   and in my dreams
   I win.
All of them are there,
   pushing me around,
   laughing at me,
   calling me names.
And I just stand there.

Quiet at first,
    letting them have their fun.
Then I stare at one of them
    and stare,
    and stare,
    and stare,
    until he asks,
    'What you starin' at?'

And then it's my turn.

I can see it in my head.
Even in slow motion,
    different camera angles.
It's brilliant!
Like an action movie!
One by one I get them
    until I'm left standing,
    and they're left bleeding.

It's an exciting dream, Lord.
But one I don't like.

I'd rather be liked.
I'd rather have more friends.
I'd rather they just left me
    alone.

But they won't.
Not until they get bored
    or I do something.

Give me courage, Lord.
Stand by me.

Amen.

—— Bruises on the inside ——

It hurts, Lord.
It hurts all over.
I can't stop it hurting.

The thing is,
    the bruises ain't too bad.
I can cope with that.
I've had bruises before.
Massive ones
    from falling out of trees,
    off of bikes
    and in to muddy puddles.
Yeah, I can deal with that.
(The grazes can be great to pick!)

But it's the inside,
    the bruises there,
    that are more difficult.
More painful.

I was in the dinner queue.
I'd picked up my tray
    and then 'they' arrived.
They just looked at me,
    whispered something
    and then pushed in.

I didn't mind that.
Everyone does it.
It's part of trying to get dinner.
But it was the rest that hurt.

First there was the insults.
Some nasty,

others rude,
    most shouted.
Everyone heard,
    everyone laughed.

Except me.

Next came the jokes
    that I didn't laugh at.
Do you know why?
Because they weren't jokes.
They were just picking on me
    because I'm new.

Why?
I'm not different,
    or weird.
They don't even know me!
Not one of them!

It's rubbish here, Lord.
I wish we'd never moved.
I wish we'd stayed where we were.
I had friends,
    places to go,
    a home.

Here?
It's all strange
    and unfriendly,
    and I wish
    I was somewhere else
    or someone else.

It hurts, Lord.
It hurts.

Amen.

—— Locker room laughs ——

Lord,
  today at school, after PE,
  everyone picked on that lad again.
I know he's annoying,
  and that he's weedy and strange,
  but today I looked at him
  and suddenly thought,
  'How would I feel?'

Why doesn't he fight back, Lord?
I know I would . . .
. . . I know I have.
But it is hard, Lord,
  in the face of such overwhelming odds.

What really upsets me, Lord,
  is that I'm afraid to help him.
I'm afraid to stand up for him.
That's not too good, is it?
But it's not right, Lord,
  and the things they call him
  and accuse him of are awful.
He's strange, Lord,
  but then aren't we all in our own little ways?
Aren't we all a bit different?

Give me courage, Lord.
Help me do the right thing
  and stop this
  not just here in the locker room,
  but out there, in the world outside.

Amen.

—— 'Pizza face! Pizza face!' ——

Lord,
   just look at me.
I mean
   how on earth
   am I,
   looking like this,
   supposed to be in anyway
   attractive
   to girls?

I know I'm only going to school
   and that today consists of
   RE (yawn),
   Physics (snore),
   and double maths (dribble),
   but I'm not even in
   with a running chance!

I look like a pizza!
No,
   I exaggerate;
I *am* a pizza.
I, a teenage lad,
   with a future,
   am nothing more
   than a colourful array
   of spots,
   pustules,
   and blackheads.

Nice.

(Not.)

So, here's a question for you, Lord.
One that I feel rather passionate about.
You see,
    I can understand why you created most things,
    but spots?
Well, I'm lost.
I mean
    why?
What is the point?
Come on!
I'm waiting for an answer!

I hate it, Lord.
I look terrible on the outside
    and this so easily makes me feel terrible
    on the inside.
I feel ugly,
    unattractive.
The ugly duckling
    destined to always be
    an ugly duckling.

You do understand, don't you, Lord?
You do realise just how important this is?
Everyone is talking about girls
    and being with girls
    and fancying girls.
I feel left out.

So and so fancies so and so,
    but no one fancies me.
I'm an all right bloke,
    but what do they care?
Who'd want to kiss me?
(And what's snogging like, Lord?)

Right, pull myself together.
It's only a day at school.
I'm off, Lord.
Out into the world,
    face cleansed and warred upon
    with the all new
    'Blackhead Busting,
    zit zapping,
    acne killer!' cream
    (that hasn't worked yet).

I know it's what's on the inside
    that counts,
    but occasionally, Lord,
    the outside matters, too.
And it's the outside
    that's worrying me.

Keep me focused, Lord,
    on what really matters.

Amen.

—— Exam time ——

Lord,
   it's started; exam time . . .
Why is it always sunny?

I'm sat here, pretending that I know
   what I'm doing
   just waiting for the time to go by
   so that I can justify going downstairs
   and having my supper.
I hate revision, Lord.
It's rubbish.

Did you ever have to revise?
Did you ever sit in front of a pile of books
   not understanding a single word within?
Isn't nice, is it?
I want to be outside or with my mates
   or anything other than this.

But if I don't do it
   where will I be then?
I'm not sure I want to go to college
   but if I don't do at least my best
   I'll be well disappointed.
Which I guess says it all.
I've got to get on with it.
The summer hols aren't that far away,
   so the question is, do I want to spend them
   feeling gutted that I didn't do my best
   or proud that I did?
The answer's simple, isn't it, Lord?

Amen.

—— Will my pen run out? ——

Lord,
    this is only going to be quick
    because I'm here,
    sat at the desk
    in a big hall full of other people
    sitting at desks.

In front of me sits
    the exam paper.
At my side
    a pile of pens,
    pencils,
    rulers,
    rubbers,
    refills
    and mints.

My only prayer,
    my only hope, Lord,
    is that I'll do my best
    and be OK
    whatever happens.

Thanks for listening, Lord.

Amen.

—— Nice 'tash'! ——

Lord,
    it's started;
    the sudden appearance
    of facial hair!
Which means only one thing . . .

. . . I need my own razor!

Ha! Ha!
'Bloke-hood' at last!
I am a man!
See my stubbly chin and furry lip!
See me bring forth my own razor,
    my own shaving gel!
See me place upon my face this cool gel
    and at last,
        take hold of my trusty weapon and

    ouch!

Oh, great, first shave
    and with it comes
    the first bunch of war wounds.
Nice.
Now I'm going to look like someone
    who has fought a razor
    rather than used one.
And none of the cuts will stop bleeding!
I thought I heard something in Biology
    about the blood having platelets
    that help it clot?
Well, there don't seem to be any in my face!

Lord,
    look at me!
So this is part of growing up too, is it?
Well, ha, ha, ha.

Right, that's it,
    done at last.
All the hair has gone
    (and there was a lot, believe me!)
    and been replaced by rather red skin
    and a few thin nicks.

So I have to do this for the rest of my life?
That's something to look forward to.
Maybe I'll just let it grow
    and have a beard.

Perhaps not.

What do you think, Lord?
Was it a good attempt
    for a first attempt?
Do I look OK?
I don't look too cut, do I?

I guess you're wondering
    why I'm telling you all this?
Well, you asked me to share everything with you.
So I am,
    shaving cuts and all!

Amen.

── Guns 'n' stuff ──

I remember when I was younger
    and playing outside in the garden
    was the best way to spend
    a Saturday.
To be honest it still is,
    but running around out back
    at my age
    would probably be a bit daft.

My favourite game
    usually revolved around getting ready
    for some kind of mission
    or adventure.
I'd been specially picked for it,
    given the details
    and been left to get ready.

It was the 'getting ready' bit
    that was the best.

I used to invent things,
    and make things
    that only a secret agent
    would have.
Mum even made me a utility belt once
    that had pockets and hooks
    and holsters and stuff.
It was ace!

I remember a gun I made once.
It was a secret one.
The kind only James Bond would be given.
I got a biro,
    a load of thin dowelling wood,

a spring,
a small piece of metal,
some glue,
a knife
and some string.

It was brilliant!
The biro case became the barrel,
    so I put the spring in
    and glued it to the stopper.
Then I filed a thin slit
    through the end of the barrel
    near the end of the spring
    that allowed me to use the piece of metal
    as a spring pull and trigger.
The thin dowelling
    was carved into a number of 'bullets',
    and the string used
    to keep the trigger in place.

The surprising thing
    is that it actually worked!
The little bits of dowelling
    shot across the garden really well!
I was chuffed to bits!

Later on I had an airgun (that was Dad's)
    and a catapult
    and my own knife.
All these 'manly' things
    that I didn't have to make
    or pretend to have any more!

You see, I was wondering, Lord,
    is it wrong to like these things?
You know, guns 'n' stuff?
I mean, I'm not obsessed or anything

but it takes a lot to beat an afternoon
of sitting out back
shooting at cans or flower pots
with an airgun or catapult.
I don't really think of them
    as weapons.
They're just something I use.

I'm probably going on and on
    about something that isn't all that important
    but I'd just like to know
    that I'm not weird,
    or evil or something.
These are dangerous things
    and I don't want to become
    obsessed
    or something.

Does this make any sense?
Probably not, Lord,
    but then you probably know
    what I'm trying to say
    even though I don't.
(Prayer's really weird, isn't it?)

So there you go, Lord;
    guns 'n' stuff.
It's on my mind
    and now I've spoken to you about it.
Don't know why really,
    other than the fact that I'm a bloke
    and I was thinking about it.

Is that OK, Lord?

Amen.

—— Top shelf ——

I'm sorry, Lord.
I couldn't help it.
I was in the newsagents,
    looking through the car mags
    when my eyes just caught
    the top shelf.

It's odd, really.
You know it's there.
You can almost sense it, as if it is looking at you,
    burning its eyes into the top of your head
    as you try your best to ignore its allure.

But occasionally,
    you fail,
    and one fleeting glance leads to another,
    and another.

It's not as though I'll buy
    one of those magazines,
    but I know someone who did.
Big lad in our year, looks eighteen,
    just picked one,
    stifled the giggles,
    handed over two quid
    and bingo!
Instant 'cool' status for eternity.
Why am I telling you this, Lord?
Well, it's just that I was thinking
    (I do occasionally)
    and it's the temptation thing that bugs me.

I'll admit, Lord,
   that I do get 'thoughts'
   about sex and stuff,
   and at times it can seem overpowering.
(The 'cold shower' idea
   is rubbish, by the way.)

And it is this feeling
   – when curiosity takes over –
   that draws my eyes to the top shelf
   to catch a glance of a naked image
   barely visible
   through a milky white half-cover,
   and I start to worry.

I want to reach up,
   and touch what I know I shouldn't.
I want to open the pages of a book
   I'm sure is best left closed,
   but at the same time
   want desperately to open.

Do you understand this, Lord?
Am I making sense?
I'm just trying to be honest with you,
   which is surely what faith is about,
   isn't it?
I know I'm no porn addict
   but I just need to know, Lord,
   that when the top shelf beckons
   and my eyes glance upwards
   I'll look that little bit further
   and see you.

Amen.

—— Strange feelings ——

Lord,
   am I normal?
I'm scared that I may not be.
That perhaps there's something
   really wrong
   with who,
   and what,
   I am.

That's what everyone would have me believe,
   anyway.
Their jokes,
   attitudes.
Not that they know I feel like this,
   'cos I have to hide what I feel,
   how I feel,
   way down deep inside me.
Then I spend day after day
   hiding behind a mask,
   the real me afraid to come out.

Not least because if I'm to believe in you
   then how I feel is wrong, too,
   and makes me a sinner.
I'm not, Lord.
I'm not dirty,
   or hideous,
   or revolting.
I'm not evil,
   or contaminated,
   or diseased.
I'm me.
Screwed up,

messed up,
and as human as the next person.

But I still feel unwanted,
untouchable.

These feelings are so hard to deal with, Lord,
even though they've always been there,
deep down.
I know it might not be the norm,
what most people feel,
but it's the way I feel,
and I always have to run away from it.

Not fancying girls isn't an easy thing to admit,
but it's true.
I never have, Lord.
Never.
Not once.
I like them,
I can see how amazing
and alluring they can be,
but to me?
Lord, it just doesn't hit home.

I'm scared to admit that I'm gay.
To openly say that I have feelings
about my own sex.
That I fancy men.
I'm so frightened that I'll lose friends,
family,
everything.
It'll all be taken away,
simply because of the way I am,
and that's not fair, Lord.
It's not fair.

I don't understand.
You created us, Lord,
   but here I am,
   created to be something that people
   ridicule,
   laugh at,
   run from
   and condemn.
How can these feelings make me a sinner?
Is it because people are afraid of me?
Of what I am?
(Even though I haven't told them yet.)

I don't know what to do, Lord.
I have all these feelings,
   all these frustrations,
   all these drives,
   and none of it makes sense.
None of it.

Do you understand, Lord?
Do you have any idea
   what is going on in my head?
The pain that I feel?
I want and need to feel loved,
   but all I feel is rejection.
I want and need to hold a hand,
   but all I feel is pushed away.
I want and need to receive affection,
   but all I feel is fear.

None of this is right, Lord,
   but I can't help who I am.
I feel lost,
   screwed up,
   rejected.

Created and then thrown on the fire.
What do I do, Lord?
There seems to be no guidance on this.
Do I come out?
Make a stand for who and what I am?
Or do I stay quiet?

Do you love me, Lord?
How can you, if what I hear is true?
That I am a sinner, born.
I've tried to rebel against these feelings,
    turn from them,
      pretend they don't exist,
      but they do.
And the longer I ignore them,
    the more difficult it gets.

Oh, Lord,
I'm so totally and utterly confused.
There seems to be no way out.
No exit,
    no escape.
But I'm not going to give up, Lord.
I'm not going to stand down.
I'm me,
    I know you love me,
    and I must hold on to that, whatever.

Stay with me, Lord,
    and hold my hand.

Amen.

—— The older woman ——

Lord,
   is this normal?
I'm supposed to fancy girls my own age,
   not their PE teacher!
But I can't help it.
She's gorgeous.
Well, at least I think so.

Is this a crush?
It's just that sounds so childish,
   and it's not like that.
Not at all.

She caught me looking at her yesterday,
   and I went bright red.
Me!
I blushed!
Can you believe it!
I mean,
   just how embarrassing is that?
She smiled,
   turned away.
But I think she knows.

I could write to her
   and tell her how I feel,
   especially as I hardly ever see her,
   seeing as she never teaches us lads.

Don't be stupid!
Who's idea was that?
I can't believe those words
   even entered my head!
Yeah, like it'd be a good idea . . .

Dear teach,
I know you're thirty five
and I know I'm a lot younger,
but I love you.
Can we give it a try?

Just how ridiculous is that?
Come on now,
back to reality;
got to concentrate on the now.
It'd never work anyway,
she likes black hair,
and I'm a blonde.

(Because *that's* why
it wouldn't work!)

This is very confusing, Lord.
Getting 'thoughts'
about someone so much older.
I don't mean to,
but they just pop in now and again.

Is that normal?
Am I normal?
I don't know.
I really don't.
I need to talk to someone about it
and you're the best there is, really,
because you won't tell
or laugh
or make me feel stupid.

I fancy an older woman.
I can hardly believe it.
But she is lovely,
and her smile . . .

Listen to me, Lord!
I'm off again!
This is not normal at all!
And apart from that,
    she's married!

Lord,
    I know I'm making jokes out of it,
    trying to laugh it off,
    but it is a serious issue at the moment.
I can't think straight,
    I can't keep my mind on my work.
I feel so confused.

I guess that's it, really;
    'confusion'.
A lack of understanding.
There's just so much going on in my head,
    and this is just another of about a million.
It hurts in here, sometimes.
I think I need a release valve
    or something,
        just to release the pressure.

Would you do that for me, Lord?
Turn the tap?

Thanks,

Amen.

— A little more personal —

This is a difficult one, Lord.
I know I'm supposed to be able
   to talk to you
   about everything,
   but some things
   are, well,
   just a little more
   personal.

Some things
   aren't meant to be spoken about.
Not seriously, anyway.
Usually it's in joke form,
   or insult, I suppose.

But I do need to talk.
It's on my mind, you see,
   and I can't help but feel
   a bit bothered about it.

Right,
   I'll get straight to the point.
No messing around,
   or moving away from the subject.
Yep,
   no problem!
After all,
   I can speak to you
   about anything,
   can't I?

Perhaps not.
Look, you know what I want to talk about,
   so why do I need to say it?

Why?
It's embarrassing!

OK,
   right,
   here goes . . .
I'll use scientific terminology
   to avoid any hint of shyness.

Masturbation.

There, I've said it!
(And I'm not saying it again).

Lord,
   is it wrong?
(This really is difficult,
   but bear with me.)
Am I stupid talking to you about it?
I hope not.

You see, I'm all a bit confused.
I don't really know
   what I want to say about it.
Well, I do,
   but it's difficult.
A bit personal.

You know what I'm trying to say, don't you?
You know what is inside my head
   trying to get out?

There's all these different issues
   tied up with it.
From lustful thoughts
   to simple sinning.
I just find it all so complicated.

Then there's the fact
   that at school
   it's always talked about,
   and not just in the playground.
We had sex education again, today,
   and the health visitor
   said that it was entirely normal
   for a teenage boy
   to 'do it'.
Said we shouldn't feel bad,
   or guilty,
   or dirty.

It's all very confusing, Lord.
I don't really know what I'm trying to say,
   so I guess all I am doing
   is talking.
Talking to you about something
   that is bothering me.
I don't expect any answers,
   or visions.
I just wanted to talk to you,
   get things off my chest.
That's OK, isn't it, Lord?

Thanks for listening.

Amen.

—— Is this normal? ——

Lord,
    I'm kind of embarrassed about this
    but I can't talk to Mum
    or Dad
    (and definitely no one else)
    about it.

You see
    I sort of,
    well you know,
    woke up
    and like,
    my bed was
    sort of,
    urm,
    well, er . . .

    (wet).

I hadn't peed myself
    or anything like that.
This was that other stuff.

Is this normal?
There seems to be so much of it
    and I'm sure I read at school
    that the average male
    only produces about a teaspoon's worth
    at a time.

It's scary, Lord.
I know that I'm supposed to be developing
    and turning into
    a 'man'

(aren't I one already?)

but this is all a bit too much
and a bit too fast.

All these things that are natural
    are for some reason
    very embarrassing.
I know they shouldn't be
    but when it's all so new
    and so strange
    and so personal
    how am I supposed to talk to anyone
    about it?

I'm facing things that are new,
    exciting,
    strange
    and scary.
Things that I have little choice
    but to go through.
I can't run away
    or pretend I'm ill,
    or stay away from school.
(Well, I could,
    but I don't think anyone
    would believe the excuse.)

Help me come to terms with this, Lord.
The changes are huge
    and my experience isn't.

Amen.

—— Adult? Me? Never! ——

Lord,
  I don't want to be one,
  an adult that is.
I know it's a long way off
  but it seems so,
  so,
  erm, er, well,
  'adult'.

I'm in my teens and know that it'll happen
  but I really don't want it to.
I'm having fun at the moment,
  I don't want all that responsibility.
The things of 'adult life'
  frighten me.
Careers, marriage,
  getting even older . . .

I'll be OK though, won't I, Lord?
It isn't as bad as it seems from here, is it?
I hope not.
But whatever it's like, Lord,
  you'll still be with me, won't you?

Thanks.

Amen.

—— What am I for? ——

Careers, Lord.
Jobs,
  occupations,
  things to do with the rest of my life . . .
  and I'm supposed to know,
  right *now,*
  what they are.

I mean *what*?
Like I have any idea?
Like I've ever really thought about it?
Well, actually, I have.
Quite a lot, too.
And it bothers me at times.

You see, Lord,
  there is all this stuff going on
  about decisions for this, that, and the other,
  and I'm pretty confused
  about the whole thing.
None of it makes sense
  and all seems such a long way away.
So, I was wondering if you could help.
You are God after all.

Lord,
  what am I here for?
What is my purpose?
What do you want me to do?
I've no idea at the moment,
  and it seems that I'm the only one at school
  who feels like this.

Everyone else seems to know already.
You know, the usual stuff:
from lawyers to electricians,
    bankers to builders,
    perhaps even simply driving a van
    (now that sounds perfect!)

Me?
Well, I'm stumped, I haven't a clue.
Finding socks in the morning
    is difficult enough
    without trying to find a career too.

I want a purpose,
I want to do something worthwhile
    and I want to be happy,
    it's just that it seems
    that I need to know all this right now
    so that I can make the right decisions
    and stuff.

Lord,
    is there any part of being a teenager
    that isn't in some way confusing,
    or annoying
    or a complete pain in the backside?

I'm sorry,
    it's just that it gets to me now and again.
(Like you hadn't already guessed that.)
I don't suppose
    you could give me a nod
    in the right direction though, Lord?
Thanks.

Amen.

The shouting downstairs

They're at it again, Lord.
Shouting at each other,
    yelling out and screaming,
    sending shock waves through the house.

It's like living in a noisy hell, Lord.

Why don't they get on?
Why don't they love each other?
And why do they keep pretending that they do?
It's not as if I believe them anymore.
I want to,
    I really do,
    but it doesn't matter how many extra
    chocolate biscuits they put in my box,
    or how many videos I'm suddenly allowed,
    I still know that they are both very unhappy.

Mum threatened to leave Dad the other night.
I heard her scream it at him,
    saying life with him was a waste of life.
He told her to leave,
    that he didn't care,
    that he wished he'd never married her.
Then they both cried,
    and everything went quiet.

Maybe they do still love each other,
    right deep down.
Maybe there is hope,
    for us as a family.
But it's hard, Lord.

What can I do?
I'm just a lad,
   nothing more, nothing less.
What can I do?

I try to help out,
   you know, smooth things over.
Perhaps help with stuff like washing up
   or tidying my room.
I tell them I love them
   and give them hugs,
   but I don't know if it's enough.

It's so hard, Lord.
There are no answers anywhere,
   no solutions to this mess in which we now live.
I just want them to love each other again, Lord.
That's all.

But what if they break up?
What then?
Lord, what do I do?
I'm so scared,
   so alone,
   so frightened.

You will stay with us, Lord,
   won't you?
No matter what happens?
I need to know that, Lord;
   that there is something stable
   in our lives.

Amen

—— I doubt it ——

Lord, I'm not too sure any more.
I'm not totally convinced.

You do exist, don't you?
I've been doing a lot of thinking recently
    and it doesn't really seem possible
    that you are there, except in my mind.

I'm not making you up, am I?
It's just that today
    one of our teachers started on
    about how there was no such thing as God,
    and how could there be,
    what with all this suffering and stuff.
You know, how could a loving God
    allow people to go through what they do?
Makes sense, I guess.
It doesn't come across as very loving.

I tried to think of a way to argue my point,
    but I didn't even put my hand in the air.
(But you know that anyway . . .
    assuming you exist, of course.)

What I want to know is,
    why it is that amongst all this doubt
    I'm still chatting to you!
Either I'm mad (and I'm not!)
    or there is something inside me . . .
    something that's got a hold of who I am
    and won't let go.
Is it your hand I feel, Lord?

Amen.

—— Puff 'n' stuff ——

Lord,
    last night, when a few of us were together,
    someone passed around a spliff.
Everyone had a toke,
    and no one went mad, or got daft,
    it just happened.

Was it wrong, Lord?
Well, I suppose it was seeing as it's illegal.
But was it wrong to be curious?
If it's any consolation
    all it did was make my head spin
    and then make me want the loo . . .
    . . . not the kind of thing I'll get addicted to.
It does worry me though, Lord.
After all, it was one of so many things to be tried
    that aren't supposed to be.

Life's difficult, Lord,
    you know that, don't you?
Not exactly the world's easiest thing.
There seem to be so many things we can do
    that are wrong,
    and I seem to have done them already!
But you do forgive me, don't you, Lord?

I'm sorry, it's just that I feel a bit down.
I'm not sure why,
    just being a teenager, I guess.
Thanks for putting up with me.

Amen.

—— To roll, or not to roll ——

Lord,
 I'm trying to think of a decent excuse for this,
 one that'll persuade you
 I didn't have much choice
 and me that it's OK.
Trouble is, I can't.

Exam pressure, revision,
 peer pressure . . .
 all rather empty really.

This is my seventh fag today,
 and it's only one in the afternoon.
Mum and Dad don't know,
 but that's probably because I eat
 about two thousand mints a day
 to disguise the smell.
And if they do ask,
 I just blame the smokers on the bus.

Why am I doing this, Lord?
It makes me look cool, I guess.
(And it does; you can't dispute it!)
I'm moving on to rollies now,
 because they look even cooler.
Well, that's what everyone else seems to think.

Am I stupid, or what?
Like this makes me look cool!
But, it's not that easy.
I can't just stop,
 put the fag out
 and never smoke again.

I'm weak, I know it,
    but at least this way people think I'm OK,
    one of 'them', one of the crowd . . .

But I don't want to be
    one of the crowd though, Lord.
That means I'm average,
    a sheep in a flock,
    happy to follow the rest.

That sounds rubbish, like I'm really weak.
Maybe I am,
    maybe that's all I will ever be.

NO!
Sack it,
    I'm not going to give in!
See this, Lord?
Behold as I stamp on this fag
    and grind it into the ground!
Watch as I walk away from it
    never to smoke again!
I don't want to be weak,
    or a faceless nobody in the crowd!
I want to be noticed, to stand out!
And it sure as heaven
    doesn't make me look cool!
But the fag . . .
No, I'm going to stop.
It's not easy,
    but I'm not going to be that easily led.
Better to start the way I plan to go on . . .
Watch me as I walk, Lord.

Amen

—— Late in ——

Lord, don't let them wake up,
    pleeeeease!
I'm a bit late, I know,
    but the extra hassle
    of a discussion at one in the morning
    about 'lack of respect'
    really isn't what I'm after.

I didn't mean to get back so late, Lord;
    it was an accident!
You know how it is
    when you're out and having a laugh;
    and the time just flies by.

They won't mind really, will they, Lord?
I understand why they worry,
    but occasionally
    it does get wearing.
I feel suffocated, and I get frustrated
    and shout and stuff.
It's not nice.

So, Lord,
    please don't let them wake up.
I'll try and be in on time
    next Friday.
Can this be between
    just you and me?
Thanks, Lord.

Amen.

—— Emergency! ——

Lord!
This is just a quick prayer,
    because I've nothing else to say
    other than
    HELP!

I can't go into it now
    because there's so much going on,
    but I just need to know
    that you're there
    beside me!

That's it!

Amen

—— Hi! ——

Lord,
  I've nothing much important to say,
  nothing terrible to moan about,
  no impending doom to ask your help for . . .
  so I just thought I'd say hi.

No reason,
  other than to let you know
  that I don't just turn up
  when things are going wrong
  or falling apart
  or I've broken up with my girlfriend
  or something.

See ya,

Amen.